Jelly and Bean live at Follifoot Farm. They have a box in the shed and a bed in the kitchen.

Wellington and Kevin live at Follifoot Farm. They have a kennel in the farmyard.

The farmer lets the dogs sleep on a rug in the kitchen in the winter.

Lotty is the farmer's pet dog. She sleeps in a basket under the kitchen table.

A family of pigs lives at Follifoot Farm. They have a hut in a pigpen in the farmyard.

Cows live at Follifoot Farm.

They stay out in the fields in the summer.

Sheep live at Follifoot Farm.

They stay up on the hill with the lambs in the summer.

The cows and the sheep live in the barn in the farmyard in the winter. Jelly and Bean often go to see them.